MONSTER AT LOCH NESS

by
Sally Berke

A

cpi

Book

RSVP
RAINTREE
STECK-VAUGHN
P U B L I S H E R S
The Steck-Vaughn Company

Austin, Texas

First Steck-Vaughn Edition 1992

Art and Photo Credits

Cover illustrations and illustrations on pages 17, 18, 19, 26, 41, and 42, Isadore Seltzer.
Photos on pages 9 and 11, Paul Hosefros/N.Y.T. Pictures
Map on page 13, N.Y.T. Pictures
Photos on pages 31 and 37, Wide World Photos
Photo on page 33, United Press International
Photo on page 39, Academy of Applied Science, Boston, Mass.
Photo on left side of page 46 and both photos on page 47, Courtesy of the American Museum of Natural History
Photo on right side of page 46, New York Zoological Society
All photo research for this book was provided by Sherry Olan.
Every effort has been made to trace the ownership of all copyrighted material in this book and to obtain permission for its use.

Library of Congress Number: 77-24715
Library of Congress Cataloging in Publication Data

Berke, Sally, 1950–
  Monster at Loch Ness

  Bibliography: p.

  SUMMARY: Discusses the legends and the evidence concerning the origins and existence of the Loch Ness monster.
  1. Loch Ness monster—Juvenile literature.
  [1. Loch Ness monster] I. Title
  QL89.2.L6B47   001.9'44   77-24715

ISBN 0-8172-1054-7 hardcover library binding

ISBN 0-8114-6858-5 softcover binding

26 27 28 29 30 W 99 98 97 96

Contents

Chapter 1

The Beginning

It was a mild summer morning. The water was calm and cool. A fisherman, ready for a pleasant day, took his boat out on the lake. About halfway across the lake, the man turned off the boat motor. He had found the perfect spot for fishing.

Suddenly, the still water began to bubble. Hundreds of tiny fish were jumping madly about the surface of the water. "What could have terrified the fish?" he thought. The man stared in wonder. Within minutes, his wonder turned to terror. He was face-to-face with the strangest thing he had ever seen!

A gray, snake-like head crept slowly out of the water. Then a long, thin neck that looked like the trunk of an elephant followed. Below that, two huge, shiny humps appeared. And the creature began to move in the water.

Fear raced through the fisherman. A chill rose up through his bones. Should he start the motor and head for land? Should he drift quietly, hoping not to be noticed? Should he scream for help? But who would hear him?

Before the man could decide, there was a loud crash of water. A storm of waves swirled around the place where the beast had risen. And, as suddenly as it had come, the creature was gone.

The fisherman started the motor and hurried his boat toward the shore. He couldn't wait to tell his friends about the creature. "But wait," he thought. "Who would believe such a tale? How could I possibly describe that beast? It looked like a dragon. No, a dinosaur. Didn't its head look something like a seal? Was it a seal? Maybe the sun was playing tricks with my eyes. Maybe I should keep the whole story to myself. Who would believe it?"

And so, the incredible beast became the fisherman's deep secret. He was afraid to tell anyone about it. It haunted him from time to time. Especially when a storm gathered over the lake. Or at night, when the waters seemed noisy.

The creature might have remained the secret of a few people like the fisherman had it not been for a story that appeared in the newspaper a short time later. COUPLE SPOTS MYSTERIOUS ANIMAL IN LOCH NESS! "It's no common animal," the story read. "It appears to be a *monster!*"

That story appeared in 1933, and since then many people have believed there is an unknown creature (or more than one) in the Scottish lake called Loch Ness. Hundreds say they've seen it, though many more have been unable to. Few agree on what it looks like. Some people have photographed a blurred object that they claim is the monster. But the pictures are so unclear that no one is sure what was photographed.

So, this strange beast has become one of the greatest mysteries in the world. If such a creature is in the lake, why isn't everyone able to see it? Why can't anyone take a clear picture of it? And if it doesn't exist—*how can so many people be mistaken?* If there is a beast in Loch Ness, what is it? Is it simply an overgrown seal? Is it a dinosaur, mysteriously hidden since prehistoric times?

Chapter 2

Home of the Legend

The watery home of the beast and its legend is in northern Scotland. It's one of the most beautiful parts of the world. The green hillsides are dotted with lakes. One of the most beautiful is Loch Ness. (The word "lake" is *loch* in Gaelic, an old language of Scotland.)

Loch Ness is long and thin—24 miles long and about a mile wide. It is the largest of the many lakes in Scotland. The loch is tucked between two mountain ranges. Steep, rocky cliffs drop straight to the water. Flowers, plants, and green trees make the area look like a fairy-tale.

For all this beauty, there is something eerie about Loch Ness. Old, crumbling castles stand along the nearby road. The most famous is the

The ancient ruins of Castle Urquhart overlook the waters of Loch Ness.

ruins of Castle Urquhart. As the morning sun rises over the water, a thick fog hangs from the sky. Low clouds cling to the mountain tops. They seem to hide some dark mystery below.

The loch is in a valley called Great Glen. Three hundred million years ago, this part of the world went through some big changes. There was a great rumbling and shaking. Then the earth split apart, and the valley was formed.

About 25,000 years ago, much of the earth was covered with mountains of ice called *glaciers*. As glaciers moved through Great Glen, they formed Loch Ness. At that time, Loch Ness was probably connected to the great North Sea. Some who believe in the monster say this is when giant beasts could have come into the loch from the sea. As the glaciers melted, they left a deposit of land that cut off the waters in the valley from the sea. Surrounded by land, these waters became a lake—Loch Ness. So, if there were monsters visiting from the sea, they were trapped, forever, in the loch.

Even the water in the loch adds more mystery to the story. The water in Loch Ness should be cold enough to freeze. But now it *never* does. (It only did so during the Ice Age.) There is often

The beautiful Loch takes on an air of calm toward evening.

much snow only 20 miles from the loch. But it *never* snows on the loch. For some unknown reason, the loch water is "different." No one really knows why it never freezes. Could it be a mysterious power lurking below the surface?

The water in the loch is thick with slime and peat. It always appears to be dark and muddy. It's almost impossible to see much of anything below a depth of about 50 feet. That's a major reason why attempts to clearly see or photograph the monster have been unsuccessful.

There are many strange tales about Loch Ness. But few are stranger than the one told about the *ghost ship of the loch*. Many villagers have claimed to have seen a large ship drifting on the loch. They say it always appears late at night. There seem to be no lights on the ship. But there is a report of a magical halo that shines on it. The ship can be seen very clearly because of this halo. Then it mysteriously vanishes.

There's more to this mystery. The ship may only be seen once every 20 years. The latest sighting was reported in 1962. In 1982, Loch-Ness-Monster-watchers may get an extra treat.

The legends surrounding Loch Ness go on and on. "The Case of the Mysterious Footprints" is another. According to the story, a holy man was preaching in the mountains near Loch Ness. The man stopped when he heard people talking in the back of the crowd. Angry, he shouted: "If I am not speaking the truth, there will be no trace of my footprints where I am standing. But if my words are true, my footprints will remain in the place for all time!"

Those prints are still in that spot today. So say many who claim to have seen them. According to these people, the footprints cannot be destroyed. Grass will not grow on them. They cannot be dug out. "Dig all you want, or try washing them away," they say. "They always reappear as clearly as before."

These Loch Ness legends of mystery have survived through the ages. But, the greatest mystery story is still the Loch Ness Monster.

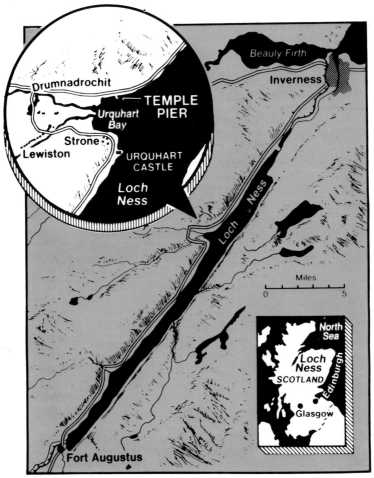

Many monster sightings have been reported along the length of Loch Ness.

Chapter 3

Tracing the Loch Ness Legend

There probably isn't anyone living near Loch Ness who hasn't heard some tale about the mysterious beast that swims in the deep, dark waters. Some choose to ignore such talk. Others can't help but wonder if there's some truth in it.

No one knows exactly when the stories began. But grandparents pass them on to their children, who later repeat them to theirs. One story is thought to go back 1400 years. It happened in A.D. 565. The story goes something like this:

St. Columba, an Irish missionary, was visiting a town near Loch Ness. On his journey, he stopped near a river and saw a group of people burying a man. St. Columba asked how the man died. "The monster," replied one of the people. "This man was snatched up by the monster."

St. Columba asked someone in the group to swim across the river and return with a boat from the other side. One man took off his clothes and jumped into the water. The splash must have scared the monster. It suddenly rose from the bottom of the water. It crashed through the surface. The beast stretched its giant mouth and let out a roar. The angry creature rushed toward the frightened swimmer. As the beast neared the man, St. Columba cried out, "Go no further nor touch that man. Go back with all speed." The monster was so frightened by the loud, fierce cry, it stopped. Then, it began swimming backwards as if it were being dragged.

Whether or not this tale is true, it is only one of many stories told about the "Monster in the Lake." No other story tells about the beast attacking a person. And only one other story says the monster makes sounds. But these stories all do have one thing in common. They all say the monster can be scared by very loud noises.

E. H. Bright, a villager, claimed he saw the Loch Ness Monster. His beast came out of the woods and waddled into the water. It looked "like an elephant." Its neck was like an elephant's trunk. To add proof to his story, Bright says he returned to the same place. This time he took his cousin. Bright pointed to the spot where he had seen the beast. There in the mud were large footprints.

These stories happened long ago. But they were kept a secret until about 50 years ago. Talking about the monster was not encouraged. In 1889, two brothers spotted a mysterious beast in the water. They dashed back to their house and told their father what they had seen. The father took his sons aside. "Never repeat this story to anyone," he warned.

It was no wonder that few people were anxious to talk about seeing a monster. People who talked of seeing huge swimming beasts were thought to be crazy.

But in time, stories of sightings have come to be widely told. They all report a strange beast in or near Loch Ness. But no two descriptions are alike. "A giant frog," says one person. "A dragon," says another. "Half-camel-half-horse," adds one more.

In 1933, a main road was built beside the loch. Did the dynamite blasting of the road crew disturb the monster? Or did the road just bring more people, more noise to the loch? We'll never know. What we do know is that in the 1930s newspapers were spreading monster stories all over the world.

One of the first news accounts told of Mr. and Mrs. John McKay. In April, 1933, the McKays were driving along the new road by Loch Ness. Mrs. McKay was looking out the window admiring the peaceful water. Suddenly, she cried, "Look, John! What's that—out there?" Mr. McKay slammed on the brakes.

Some people have said the monster looks like a frog.

Some claim the monster is half horse, half camel.

Out in the lake was the strangest thing they had ever seen. A huge animal was rolling and diving in the loch. The McKays had hardly stopped the car when there was a loud splash. The animal plunged beneath the surface. As quickly as it had appeared, it was out of sight.

The McKays told their friend Alex Campbell about the beast. Campbell, a newspaper writer, wanted to report the story. He gave it to the editor of the *Inverness Courier*. The editor replied, "If it's as big as Campbell says, we can't just call it a creature. It must be a *monster*."

On May 2, 1933, the story appeared in the *Courier*. Many say this story began the world-wide interest in the Loch Ness Monster.

Other newspapers hurried to print stories of the monster. News at the time was gloomy. The world was on the brink of war. The excitement of a monster story was a welcome change. The reports from the *Daily Express* in Glasgow, Scotland appeared every couple of weeks!

By October, 1933, over 20 people said they had seen the monster. Newspapers began sending reporters to the loch. These reporters talked to the eyewitnesses. The monster at Loch Ness became so popular it was playfully named "Nessie." Radio programs were even interrupted with news bulletins from the loch.

But all the interest in Nessie presented a new problem. Her life was now in danger. Someone might try to steal, hurt, or kill her. Five constables (police) were sent to watch the loch and protect the monster.

The police protection was not a silly idea. Many people wanted the beast out of the loch. Bertram Mill's Circus was offering a large reward for the live capture of the monster. So was the New York Zoological Park.

Many people, including scientists, thought the excitement was uncalled for. For them, there was no mysterious creature. But what about the reports? "Just a clump of weeds," said one scientist. "Just a white whale," said another. The scientists demanded more proof. That led to the next step in the Loch Ness investigation.

Chapter 4

Eyewitness Reports from the "Monster Spotters"

From St. Columba's time to the present there have been more than 10,000 reported sightings of the Loch Ness Monster. Only about 3,500 of these were written in any detail. Many of the reported objects turned out to be logs, birds, and waves. Scientists are careful about which reports they rely on.

William Akins, a Loch Ness scientist, listed the requirements of what he thought made a good report:

- The people who saw the beast
- Where the people saw the monster
- How far they were from the beast
- The date and hour of the sighting
- How long the sighting lasted
- The conditions during the sighting
- Details of what the beast looked like

Akins didn't use the reports of eye witnesses if the beast appeared for less than ten minutes. He also thought reports on clear days were more accurate than those on cloudy days.

The following reports are considered good scientific sightings:

On August 11, 1933, A. H. Palmer was camping by the loch. At 7:00 A.M., Palmer heard a strange noise. At first, he thought the wind was howling. He got up and walked toward the shore. The trees around him were very still. He looked onto the water. It was foaming and churning. An hour later, the water was calm. Palmer thought the incident was over. But then he saw something in the water, about 100 yards away. It was the head of an animal! Its mouth opened and closed. The mouth looked about 12 to 18 inches long and opened 6 inches wide. Two antennae stuck out of the head. Palmer watched for about 30 minutes. Then it disappeared.

Brother Richard Horan of St. Benedict's Abbey in Fort Augustus also gave an important report. In May, 1934, Brother Horan was working near the shore of the loch. Suddenly, he heard a crash of waves. Brother Horan looked up. Swimming 30 yards away, was a nasty-looking beast. Brother Horan reported that the head looked like that of a seal. It had no ears, and it's neck was three and one-half feet long with a white stripe down the front. As the beast moved, it kept changing direction. At one point, a row boat moved into its path. The beast stopped swimming and began kicking up the water. After a few seconds, the creature began paddling away. Finally the beast dove underwater and was gone.

Another amazing report came from Mrs. Greta Finlay. She told her story to author Constance Whyte. It appears in her book, *More Than a Legend*. The Finlay family was on vacation. Their trailer was parked on the loch near Tor Point. Mrs. Finlay and her son, Harry, were making lunch. Suddenly, a great splash came from the loch. The Finlays raced to the water. They were shocked to see what was lying on the shore. "An enormous snail," is how Mrs. Finlay described it. She explained that the ugly animal looked about 15 feet long. It had two or three humps. The head and neck were two and one-half feet long. Mrs. Finlay reported that the straight neck was attached to a bulky body. There were six-inch-long "things" sticking out of the head. Each had a blob on the end. The animal appeared to have black, shiny skin.

These reported sightings were all made while the monster was in the water. But some eyewitnesses claim to have seen Nessie on land.

There have been detailed reports of the monster being sighted on land. In 1919, the Loch Ness Monster turned a pleasant Sunday outing into an unforgettable experience for a group of children. A few years ago, Mrs. Margaret Cameron told the story to author Nicholas Witchell.

Mrs. Cameron was a child at the time. She, her brothers, and her sister were playing by the loch. Mrs. Cameron recalled: "We were waiting for some friends and were passing the time by skimming stones across the water. We heard this awful crackling in the trees on the other side of the little bay.

"It must have been something awfully big, we thought. Of course, we had been warned not to go near the loch by our grandparents, as there were these wild horses in the loch. We thought this must be one of them.

"So we sat for a wee while and this crackling seemed to be coming nearer and nearer. Then, suddenly, this big thing appeared out of the trees and started to move down the beach to the water. I couldn't tell you if it had a long neck or a short neck because it was pointing straight at us. It had a huge body, and its movement as it came out of the trees was like a caterpillar. I would say it was a good 20 feet long—what we saw of it. Now, the color of it—I hadn't seen an elephant in them days. But its color seemed like that of an elephant. It seemed to have rather a shiny skin. Under it we saw two short, round feet at the front. It lurched to one side and put one foot into the water. Then the other one. We didn't wait to see the end of it coming out—we got too big a fright.

"When we got home we were all sick and couldn't take our tea. So we had to explain what had happened. We told our mum and dad. I can see our grandfather banging on the table, telling us not to tell anybody about it. Anyway, we were put to bed with a big dose of castor oil. It still is so very vivid in my mind. I'll never forget it."

Could it have been the Loch Ness Monster—*out of the loch*? Mrs. Cameron waited many years to tell her story. Possibly some facts were twisted or forgotten. Maybe the imaginations of children were at work. But the story can't be dismissed. It is *only one* of the many land sightings. Could this be a new clue? Not only does Nessie seem to live in the loch, but she may also stroll along the beaches and roads. There were more reports of land sightings.

It was 5:00 in the morning in the year 1923. Alfred Cruickshank was driving his Model T car down the old north shore road. It was still dark and the Model T's headlights shed a dim light on the hilly road ahead. As the car reached the top

The monster is believed by some people to look like a dragon.

of a hill, the shadow of a beast plodded onto the road. Cruickshank was stunned. The large, hump-bodied beast looked about six feet tall. It didn't have much of a neck, according to the report. Its head sat right on top of its body. Its belly dragged on the ground, followed by a long, thick tail. The creature waddled away from the road, and Mr. Cruickshank slowly drove on. As he rounded a corner he heard a grunting noise, so he stopped the car to get a look. But the animal had disappeared into the water.

Could such a sighting be true? Did Mr. Cruickshank see the Loch Ness Monster? Perhaps the dim headlights of the Model T played games with the shadows of trees. What of the "grunting noises"? No other reports, except St. Columba's story, tell of any noise. A mistake by Mr. Cruickshank, or a new clue?

Ten years later, one of the most famous land sightings took place. It was late afternoon, July, 1933. Mr. and Mrs. George Spicer were driving back from vacation on the shore road. The ride was quiet until Mrs. Spicer cried out, "What on earth is that?"

Out of the bushes waved an elephant-like trunk. It was followed by a huge, clumsy body. Was it the Loch Ness Monster?

The creature lumbered across the road. It was so large that it took up the whole road. As the Spicers watched in amazement, the animal disappeared into the loch.

The Spicers drove on until they met a man on a bicycle. They stopped him and told him about the beast. They feared that he would not believe such a story. But this was the second time this man had heard about the beast. "My friend also saw it," he said. "But people are laughing at him back at the village." The man jumped on his bicycle and rode back to where the Spicers saw the beast. There, he later reported, the grass and bushes were flattened out "as if a steamroller had been through." *More proof?*

Eyewitness reports give many clues about the monster. But the reports don't agree. Does the beast have one hump or three? Does it have feet to walk on land or a flipper to swim in the water? *Or both?* Is it black or gray? Is the skin smooth and shiny, or bumpy? Does it have a long neck, or no neck at all? Only a few people saw two antennae on its head. Only two reports tell of a noise. What can be believed from all the eyewitness reports? Were some people mistaken? If so, which ones? Are there *many* monsters that look different from each other?

Chapter 5

What Does the Monster Look Like?

Luckily there is another way to study the beast. This way doesn't depend only on the eyes and mind of a person. A picture is worth more than a thousand words. Scientists wanted the monster photographed.

But that was easier said than done. A clear photograph of the beast has been hard to get. Most pictures are a fuzzy blur. Often the photographer is too far away for a clear picture. The water in the loch is too murky for a good underwater shot. What's worse, many pictures turn out to be fakes. Here's an example:

In 1960, a photo by Peter O'Connor made a big hit in the *Weekly Scotsman*. O'Connor told how he took the picture. He claimed he was camping near the loch. He awoke just before dawn and walked to the shore. There, he said, he saw the beast. O'Connor crept into the water and snapped its picture.

Many experts did not believe O'Connor's photo nor his facts. The size of the animal seemed out of scale with the distance from which O'Connor claimed he took the picture. One critic set out to prove O'Connor's picture was a fake.

Two weeks after O'Connor's "monster picture" was taken, the critic investigated the spot where O'Connor said he had been. There he found three large plastic bags. He also found some stones and a stick. Putting all the items together, the critic realized he was on to something. He blew up the bags, weighted them with stones, and stuck the stick on top. He took a picture of this contraption. The results looked like the "monster" in O'Connor's picture.

In April, 1934, Dr. R. Kenneth Wilson took the best known photo of the beast. Dr. Wilson was a London surgeon vacationing in Scotland. Early one morning he was driving along the road by the loch. Wilson looked out on the lake and saw the water churning. Then suddenly he saw the head and neck of the beast. Wilson ran for his camera and took four shots. He dashed to the local drugstore to have the photos made. Only two came out. But they gave the world the clearest monster pictures to date. His famous pictures are, to this day, known as the "surgeon's shots."

The first picture showed a long, graceful neck with a small head. Around the base of the neck were small ripples in the water. Some experts say this could be caused by the flippers or tail of the animal.

The second picture was hazier than the first. But it seemed to show the top of the neck and head. It was taken just before the animal plunged into the water. Were these photos at

Taken in 1934, this photo by Dr. R. Kenneth Wilson shows the monster's head and neck rising out of the water.

last proof to the world that there was a beast in Loch Ness?

Dr. Wilson's photos have been examined by many experts. Most agree that the photos have not been faked. Others, however, insist that Wilson's pictures show merely a floating log, or the tail of a diving otter, or the fin of a killer whale.

Despite his critics, Dr. Wilson's photos have become famous. People had waited a long time for this kind of proof. At last Nessie seemed real. Almost overnight, Loch Ness' towns were flooded with visitors. People who lived there turned their homes into restaurants. There was hardly a city or town in all that part of Scotland where people didn't ask, "What is Nessie?"

The excitement lasted about five years. Then World War II began. War stories filled the news. There were few sightings of the monster. Nessie seemed all but forgotten. Did she return to the depths for good? Or had people lost interest in looking for her?

The mystery dramatically reopened in 1960. This time it was 50 feet of film that made the news. The man with the camera was Tom Dinsdale. He believed Nessie was real and was

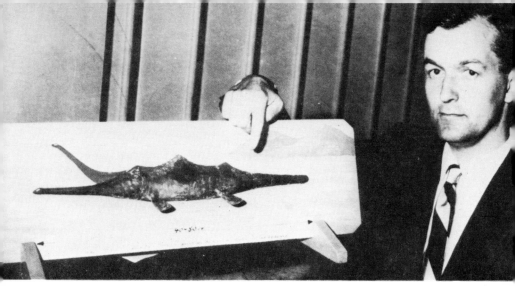

Tom Dinsdale displays a model of the monster
he saw swimming and diving in 1960.

eager to prove it. For months, Dinsdale made
trips to the loch. He wrote down everything he
saw. He kept his camera always handy, waiting
for the great moment. That moment finally came
during a five-day watch on the loch.

It was Saturday, the fifth day. The beast had
not yet shown itself. Dinsdale was getting used
to disappointment. It was early morning, but
Dinsdale already felt the day was a waste of
time. He decided to drive back to his hotel for
breakfast. With one eye on the road and the
other peering through the trees at the water,
Dinsdale drove slowly around the loch. Suddenly something in the loch caught his eye.

Dinsdale pulled the car to the side of the
road. He jumped out and grabbed his field glas-

33

ses. Sure enough, there was something quite large lying still in the water. Was it a log? Or Nessie? Dinsdale saw ripples floating to the sides of the object. The "something" was alive!

Quickly Dinsdale set up his camera. He filmed the beast as it swam across the loch. For four minutes, Dinsdale's camera caught the motion of the mysterious creature. But now he was running out of film. Should he stay there until the film ran out? Or should he save the film and try to drive closer to the animal? Dinsdale took a chance. He raced his car across a field to the edge of the loch. But his plan failed. When he got to the water, the beast was gone.

But Dinsdale had his 50 feet of film. Though taken from some distance, it did show a moving body in the water.

The film reached the scientific world quickly. Experts checked it frame by frame. Most agreed that Dinsdale *had* photographed the humped back of a living creature. But others still have their doubts.

What was needed was a better planned, more accurate photograph. And that's what came next.

Chapter 6

The Underwater "Hunt"

Nessie's next big show was photographed by Robert H. Rines and his crew. This time the pictures were taken from *under the water.*

In 1972, Rines and his crew set up lights, cameras, and sonar equipment on two boats. Sonar is a device that can locate objects underwater by means of sound waves. The machine sends out a sound wave. When the sound wave makes contact with an object, the size and motion of the object registers on the sonar monitoring screen.

Here's what Rines *hoped* would happen: The sonar would register when Nessie passed near the boats. This contact would trigger the lights. The lights would brighten the murky waters enough for a picture to be taken. Then the cameras would snap pictures. That was the plan.

Here's what *did* happen: Late one August night, the crew set out in two boats. One boat, the *Narwhal* had the sonar equipment. The other boat, the *Nan,* had the camera. The *Narwhal* crew lowered the sonar box into the water. They watched a sonar screen for signs of underwater life. The water seemed normal. There were the usual small dots floating across the screen—signs of fish.

In the quiet night air, two crew members fell asleep. Another kept her eye on the screen. Suddenly, she shouted, "Something's happening!" The others awoke. The dots were no longer floating across the screen. They had become long streaks of light. The fish seemed to be racing away from something.

Then a big black trace appeared on the screen. Peter Davies, skipper of the *Narwhal,* told this story to author Nicholas Witchell:

"To begin with, we thought it must be two or three fish close together. But then it got bigger and blacker and thicker. We could hardly believe our eyes. Something huge was moving down there, very near to where the camera was. We watched it in silence for a moment. The size of it was so large in comparison with the fish. It appeared to be moving slowly, but the trace kept coming on."

Davies then got into a smaller boat. He paddled toward the *Nan* to tell Rines and the others. He recalled, "I don't mind telling you that it was rather a strange feeling rowing across the pitch-black water, knowing that there was a very large animal 30 feet below.

Davies picked up Rines and another crew member and took them back to the *Narwhal.*

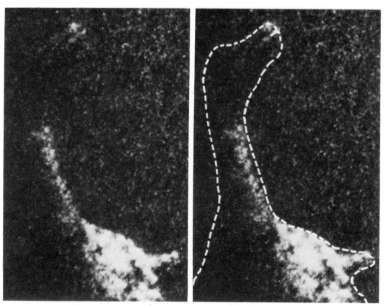

This underwater photo by Charles Wyckoff shows the outline (in white) of a creature in Loch Ness.

Everyone sat in front of the sonar screen. *The next few moments could change their lives!*

The trace on the screen was getting bigger. By now there were no fish around. Suddenly the water began to roar. Lights flashed. Cameras clicked. Would this moment convince the world that the monster lives?

The photos were far from perfect. The murky water blurred the creature. But one photo did give some important clues. It showed a fin connected to a body. The fin appeared to be between six and eight feet long. It was probably two to four feet wide. Most experts agree that this animal is different from any known.

In June, 1975, Rines and his staff returned for more pictures. Cameras and lights were fixed firmly to avoid as much floating peat as possible. Then, something strange happened to disturb the camera. Some now guess that an animal stirred up the water and knocked over the camera. But, as it was knocked about, the camera somehow still snapped pictures. As it tumbled, it shot a picture of the bottom of the boat. It also got a picture of whatever had knocked it over. Was it the monster? The body of this creature seemed about 20 feet long, with a 7 foot neck.

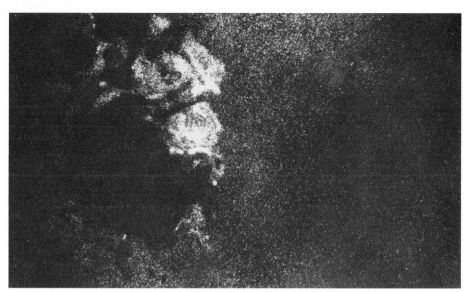

In 1975, Rines took this underwater photo of what seems to be the head of the monster.

Rines' photos were too fuzzy to convince many experts that any kind of beast was photographed. But Rines did not give up. In 1976, he and his crew again returned to Loch Ness. This time the cameras found something new. Lying on the lake floor was a skeleton of some kind of animal. The animal seemed to have a long neck and a roundish body.

The use of sonar equipment is the newest and, some say, the best way of studying the beast. Sonar charts show that there are large, moving objects in the loch. This seems to say that there is more than one beast. The beasts seem to live along the bottom and sides of the loch. They appear to move quickly—as fast as 17 miles per hour!

Chapter 7

How Do You Catch A Monster?

Scientific methods are usually the best way to get information. Yet, none has proved what lies beneath the surface in Loch Ness. From time to time, people have tried all sorts of unscientific ways to study the monster. Who's to say that one of these methods won't turn up the Loch Ness Monster?

In the summer of 1976, a few people tried to tempt Nessie's taste buds. These people went up in a balloon. They drifted over the loch, waving a hunk of bacon from a rope. The plan failed to arouse Nessie. She may not have been in the water. She may not have cared for bacon. Or she may have seen the bacon, thought of snatching it, and decided not to risk giving away her secret. We'll never know. We do know Nessie

Nessie didn't bite when these people went fishing from
a balloon, using bacon as bait.

41

Even this "friend" for Nessie failed to lure the monster
from the murky depths of Loch Ness.

didn't bite. She left the tired ballooners to "bring home the bacon" themselves.

Project "mate-a-monster" also failed to stir Nessie out of the water. Some joke players rigged up a friend for Nessie. The fake monster had flashing green eyes and long, curly eyelashes—a real "beauty!" Two fireman rode on her, yelling a "monster mating call." Needless to say, Nessie just wasn't interested.

On the serious side, some people want to capture the beast. They feel that since there are probably many monsters, one should be caught and studied.

Although scientists want to learn more about Nessie, they also want to keep her alive. Until they find a foolproof way to study her in *our* environment, they will keep on trying to study Nessie in *hers*.

Chapter 8

What Is the Monster in the Lake?

You've read some of the facts. Do you believe there's a monster in Loch Ness? If you
don't, you're not alone. Some critics say the
monster is just a publicity stunt to drum up busi-
ness around Loch Ness. But the monster tales
were around long before the tourists started to
come.

Maybe *you* believe there's a strange beast
in Loch Ness. The next question is: What is it?
Everyone seems to have an idea. From reports
and photos, we can put together this kind of
description: The monster's body is from 20 to 50
feet long. It has a long neck with a small head
attached. The body appears to have one or more
humps. The creature also has a tail about six feet
long. Most agree it is dark in color and moves
quite fast.

Most scientists feel there is probably a whole family of beasts in the loch. This would explain all the different descriptions. It also explains how sightings occur at the same time at different places.

The next question is harder to prove: What *kind* of animal is down there? Is it a new kind of familiar animal like a seal or otter? Is it a mysterious relic from the dinosaur age? More frightening, is it a creature that has never before been known to the world?

Maybe the beast is a giant seal with an unusually long neck and tail. Seals are known to dive as deep as the beast in the reports. Seals can also live in the water temperature of the loch. One kind of seal, the elephant seal, is as large as the smallest reported size of the monster. The seal theory has one problem. Seals bear their young on land. If the monster is a seal, why haven't there been more land sightings?

Maybe the beast is a kind of fish. Some people have guessed a giant salmon, eel, or shark. This would explain how the beast lives underwater. But the size and movement of these fish are not at all like the monster's.

45

Plesiosaur

Elephant seal

As strange as it sounds, the Loch Ness Monster seems most like a kind of dinosaur. A fish-eating, sea-living dinosaur, called *plesiosaur*, is believed to have become extinct 70 million years ago. The plesiosaur is known to have been 50 feet long. It had a long neck, small head, flippers, and a hump.

So, do we have our answer? Is the Loch Ness Monster a kind of dinosaur? If this is the answer, there are a hundred more questions. How did the beast live when the rest died off 70 million years ago? This would not be the first animal that has done something like this. In 1938, and again in 1952, a five-foot long fish, called coelacanth, was found. This kind of fish was believed to have been extinct for 70 million years.

The dinosaur theory does have some holes in it. Maybe some plesiosaurs lived through the extinction of the family. But none could have lived through the Ice Age. No animal could have lived in the loch when it was pure ice. There are also many differences between the monster and the ancient plesiosaur. For example, the plesiosaur swam near the water surface because it needed air. This monster does not. Also the plesiosaur could not live in water as cold as the loch.

People who believe the plesiosaur theory have an answer. At the time of the plesiosaur, there were no humans. The closest thing to a human was a mouse-like creature. This creature evolved into a human in 70 million years. Why couldn't the plesiosaur have evolved into the present day creature that lives in Loch Ness?

Otter

Coelacanth

So far, we cannot say for certain that the monster belongs to any of these groups. Perhaps when more information is gathered, we will be able to say it is a fish, or seal, or dinosaur. Or perhaps with more study we'll find the beast belongs to no known animal group. If this is true, the mystery may last forever.

Meanwhile the search for answers goes on. Sonar silently scans the depths of the loch. Photographers peer out at the surface hoping for the one clear "monster shot." In the towns around the loch, people repeat tales as old as St. Columba's. Visitors drive in for a day or two to share in the excitement. They drop by shops to buy a plastic model of the monster. Or they stop at a food stand for a "Monster-burger."

And somewhere in the depths of the black, murky water is the creature known as the Loch Ness Monster. Or is there?

Mystery still plays a wonderful role in this world. It brightens our lives by giving our imaginations something to play with. Maybe we don't really want to solve this mystery. Maybe we simply *need* to believe that there is some unexplained beast swimming in the darkness of Loch Ness.